Consequently

Dedication

To anyone who willingly reads this,

I am grateful.

Acknowledgements

When this was only a dream,

only you

made the effort to help me transform it into a reality.

Ashley Negron

I love you.

Brushstrokes

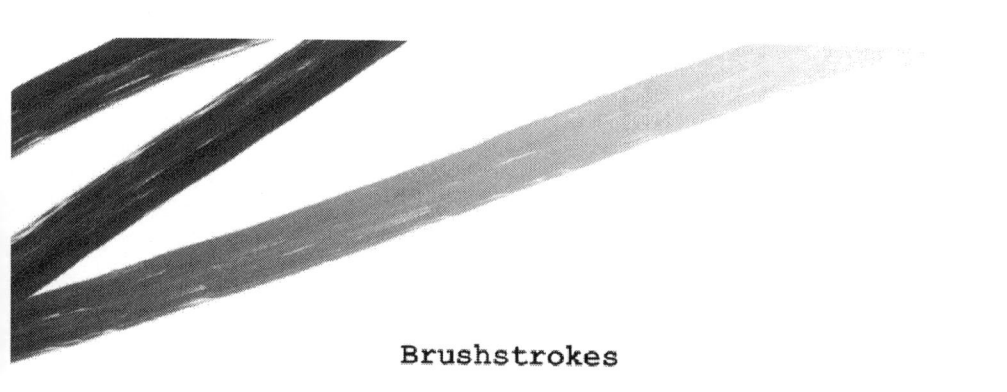

My Thoughts are like Picasso paintings
You have to stare at them a while
to know what your really looking at to understand them.

Not done yet...

I spoke to her over the phone exactly one minute ago.
She has the most incredible way
Of manipulating my lips even from far away,
to make them curl into a smile with just the sound of her voice.
I close my eyes and try to picture her laying next to me on this bed.
Telling me what she has to say
 but right here as if we were about to call it a night together.
She can tell im tired
but knows I won't say goodnight because these moments are precious between us.
Long distance has a way of giving you perspective
on what quality time can be with a person you love.
She asks me how my day was.
And I can tell she's smiling now too
As I talk to her about my evening and my feelings for her.
But time is never sufficient
and when less desired, we agree to hang up.
Not before she ceremonially showers me with the sound of her kisses.
Muah, Muah , Muah, Muah,...
I follow suit, and return the gesture.
"Alright my love, Goodnig--..."
I began to initiate the parting words when abruptly she adds:
"I'm not done yet!"
She blesses with me more kisses ... muah muah muah
Our parting words are said.
and now the conversation can end.
I hung up a minute ago,
And I'm still smiling...I guess im not done yet.

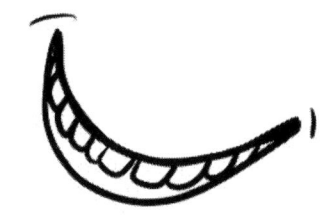

Reminder

Sometimes I forget that Poetry is not about
Structured sentences, unique vocabulary
Or even clever thoughts.
When I look in the mirror every morning before work,
That
Is poetry.
Just think about it,
I'm a metaphor for people who can't read.

Dead People

A bee dies
every time it uses it's stinger.
I wonder how would it work

If people did the same thing
When they fall in and out of love.

A stinger for a heartbreak
How many dead people would we see?

Consequently

I once heard a preacher say
that we are all the Sum total
Of our existence.
Who you are,
Is a complete record of all that has influenced you.
If that is the case,
I am a 1973 Fania All Star Salsa Record I heard while hiding in my room from my evangelical parents with my earbuds on low.
I am a 1992 Honda Prelude bought cash to be my ride for my first year of college.
I am a bottle of Malta India, the one that I drank on my 21st birthday to celebrate at the beach with my family and friends.
I am that failing academic notice letter I received for doing horribly my last semester in Marriage and Family class.
I am that argument I had with my parents about the failing academic letter.
I am that preacher man I heard. His words really got to me. After a couple of rough years, I thought I'd be better off practicing what He preached. Life is better now. Thankfully.
I am Univision, specifically Sábado Gigante with Don Fransico.
I am all of Pablo Neruda's poems. Actually you can throw in Bukowski, Whitman and Jose Marti in here too.
I am the Mofongo my dad makes to entertain guests that travel to see us as a family.
I am the taste of Passion Fruit.
I am an ENFJ according to the Meyers-Briggs.
I am the $4,000 Electric Keyboard my parents bought me when they were financially struggling to support my aspiration of becoming a professional Musician for my church. By the way, I am now.
I am Mr.Nazario (coolest algebra teacher), Mrs.Barquero (English), Ms.Ambros (Geography) and Mr.Rossi (Music).
After all that, there is still so much more
to eventually be added and applied.
This list will continue to grow
and consequently so will I.

Conquistadores

You really want to start a fight with me?
Did you not know,
my ancestors were conquistadores.
They were revered as gods with the firepower they could unleash.
Civilizations were crushed at their will
Nations birthed by their might.
So go ahead, provoke me.

Commander

Life is a battleground
that few men can go fighting
without sustaining injury.
All men are enlisted in this war,
yet only a distinct few are positioned
to spark the flame of inspiration
In others to push onwards.
When He speaks,
you can smell lavender in air.
His eyes are piercing to the soul,
No blade is as sharp as his gaze.
He stands firm in addressing adversity,
His legs are braced with steel, they will not strain with stress.
Those who aspire to leadership
Find it in his shadow.
Those who yearn for order
Receive it in his instruction.
The ones who seek to be honored,
Learn to Honor his legacy.
He believes that service is not a platform for greatness,
But to serve is greatness.
He may be called by many names:
Father, Mentor, and Friend
In this battle we call life,
We all have a Commander.

For my wife although I'm not married yet.

What the hell took you so long!
Im sorry honey, the wait felt like forever.
You see,
I've wasted a large part of my 20s to women who don't measure up to half the woman you are.
Granted, I wasn't quite ready either with all my insecurities.
I thought you were coming sooner so I was too eager waiting for a knock on my door than actually preparing for your arrival.
I'm Good now though.
The fact your here now makes me so happy.
You know that moment when you eat a warm chocolate chip cookie and then sip that cold glass of milk?
That's the type of happy I am with you as my wife.
Oh! You know how you feel when a friend hands you a starburst and they give you the pink one…
That's How It is knowing you are my wife.
Honey, I am going to love you the same way Disney loves tourists.
Doing all sorts of crazy things just so that they can have a magical time having fun.
Baby, and just like the first time we did fireworks together and afterwards I burned your father's garage door,
our marriage is going to be awesome with lots of stories to talk about along the way.
Thank you for saying "yes" and "I do".

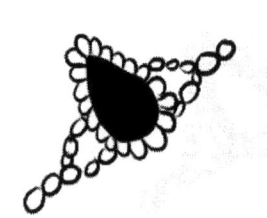

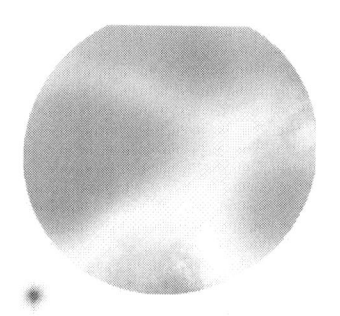

Dream

```
Along the path I stride.
Each step longer than
The next.
Slowly, I am there.
HERE!
Fast, Asleep.
Rest
Breathe
AWAKEN
```

Sunflower Seeds

I deal with my problems like
how I eat Sunflower seeds.
No matter how big is the bag,
I only eat one at a time

But Think ..

Some Days you can't
Help but think.
Life, love, the future,
Past , poetry , light
Black, blue and red
Wonderful things
Sad things
Great things
All things
They are my things.

Baggage Claim

I travel often,
the part I dread most is baggage claim.
It is an uncomfortable ceremony that creates anxiety in people like me.
Eyes constantly searching, hands eagerly ready to reunite with what you parted with.
A buzzer sounds and the ritual begins.
The carousel sorrowfully hums
and the gathering slowly happens.
Everyone is now with a heightened state of vigilance.
The bags start to make their entrance through the curtain,
A purple case labeled " Daddy issues" passes by, a pregnant 24 year old asks if I can take it off the track for her.
I do, cautiously.
I wonder for a moment where she might be going.
Then an older gentleman mid 50s I'd say, pardons his reach as the black bag he pulls off visibly reads "Unfulfilled Dreams".
I hold my place in line as now more and more baggage is being pushed out from the curtain
I can't help but continue reading the tags as they make their way past me:
Depression
       Divorce
              Anxiety
                       Debt
There were quite a few that were labeled trust issues and others simply bad temper
Each one being claimed then solemnly dragged away.
Finally, I see my suitcase
And just like the others, I check the tag to make sure it's mine.
Regret
I take it off the carousel and while another traveling stranger takes my spot in line
I walk away to call a taxi outside.
Once I get home I just want to unpack.
I tell myself again , I hate baggage claim.

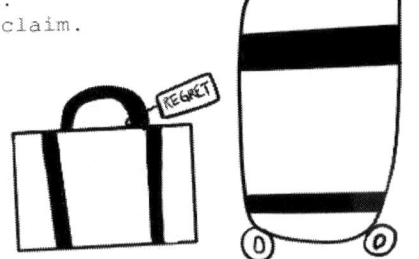

Lowered Expectations

She walked past me in a hurry.
Excuse me ma'am,
I think you dropped this…
My hands reach out
lifting up her lowered expectations.
She seemed surprised that a man cared
enough to bring them back up from
where another had apparently loosened
them.

Dramatic

After class he passed her a note
Can I be your Romeo?
She raised an eyebrow and scribbled back
I won't play dead for you
and *Don't expect me to cry afterwards
when you kill yourself for me.*

Theater kids are so dramatic.

Love God Love People

Christ had one message
As he spread wisdom on this earth
Love God Love People
Simple Words of Worth

All are bound to Serve a master
You choose at your will
Love God Love People
Its action not a skill

This doesn't require a diploma
There's no fee for initiation.
Love God Love People
It's to Show Respect and Appreciation

Life is full of moments
Never take one for granted
Love God Love People
Be rooted, stay planted.

This is my life's motto
My mission and my creed
Love God Love People
Shackled once, now I'm freed.

Library

Amidst the old,
One breathes the new.
Weary yet one finds rest.
Scattered knowledge surrounds me,
And I..
What could I offer to these renditions,
Of penned Gold.
Time seems to have melted in suspension.
Ideas being transcribed into the fabric of one's
mind.
Here I sit, contemplating
In the presence of
Eternal works of genius.
This is more than a library.
This a mecca of gathered thoughts.
All at my disposal,
Do I dare to reach and expose them?

The letter a student wrote me

My mom told me she dont want me in her house
No more
She doesn't want to know about me
No more
And I can't have her number
No more
And she said that she didn't care if I say
I love you
No more
But
I guess I just had to tell you because
I couldn't hold this in
No more.

HEROES

I used to teach all about heroes.
Mythological ones
Historical ones
The modern day super citizen heroes, the ones
you have to do a project for in Civics Class.
If I can be transparent,
I get it.
Hooray for the human race.
But where did they all go?
When did all the hero's die out?
I've been reading the papers and it seems like
the villains always get the cover story now.
There was a time where heroes were sought
after.
Was it our fault?
Did we expose our future generations to the
idea that dragons and brave knights were not
real?
Did we unintentionally guide our children to
only save themselves and not to care about the
sufferings of others?
Did we unknowingly highlight the defeats of men
on influential platforms
and create a veil to no longer witness acts of
greatness by everyday common men?
Someday the heroes might come back...
With how things are now,
I pray that it is soon.

The Captain

Allow me to enlighten you,
My classroom
is the equivalent of a pristine maritime vessel headed
towards waters of yearlong educational uncertainty.
I have set a course which I charted myself
Hours of lesson planning reviewing the most productive
routes of success.
My crew can be cautious of authority,
any amount of trepidation on my part can cause a mutiny.
At last All is well,
with me they do not have the satisfaction of being without
direction.
There is clarity of Leadership here.
On this ship there is no room for complacency. All hands
must be on deck.
The journey is relentless,
but so am I.
The relationship I cultivate with my crew is the treasure
they value most through our adventure.
That is why they will navigate and attend to the sails of
academic assessments with ease.
I have prepared each one to the best of my capabilities on
their potential and prowess.
If at the year's end, our course runs true
My crew will have finally arrived.
And it will be my honor to let them disembark and
celebrate.
While I will remain on board
to await the next journey
with eager new sailors.
And Once again Introduce myself as
Their Captain.
(Anchor)

Hot Sauce

I put too much hot sauce in my soup
My lips feel like they are pulsating,
Throbbing to the marching beat of a war drum.
My breathing changes,
My lungs expand slower to see if exhaling softly gives me some relief.
I'm sweating now too...
this is embarrassing.
It's the same way I felt when I first kissed her.
It was hot that day.
We called for an Uber after seeing the animals at the zoo
and it was only our 1st date.
We sat tightly pressed against one another,
That's when we both knew you had telepathy,
You knew exactly what I was thinking.
Just by acknowledging my eyes you agreed to it.
We gently kissed.
Thinking it through
It was better than What I put in this soup.

LDR

Love takes time,
dedication & persistence.
And I promise to love you,
even at a distance.'

I know love has no measure.
Be it in inches, meters or miles.
I'll do anything to love you,
Just to see you smile.

Our relationship is based on core values;
Loyalty, Fidelity, Trust
Placing faith in the center
It's incorruptible, stainless, no rust.

At long last my darling,
Although I've not seen you today.
My love will always reach you
No matter how far away.

????

When did it happen?

How could that be?

What was I thinking?

Who told you that?

Where is the restroom?

We ask so many questions.
Just wondering…

Why?

The Musician

I was about 9
When I first began learning about music.
Listening to the sweetness
of each note I heard
Becoming mesmerized
by the way musicians performed so effortlessly on the stages I casually passed by.
The greatest musician I ever knew
Was a 17 year old girl I dated once
She played me so well...
The song she performed I believe
Was in a minor key.
I know that because It felt dark and depressing afterwards.
It was like a symphony really.
There were multiple instruments involved.
Those guys were unaware of each other's specific parts in the score she wrote.
Hands down, she was talented.
At the end of it,
There was a standing ovation.
I looked around and she took a bow
And left the stage.
To this day,
She's still the greatest musician, I've ever seen perform.

10 things I wished I could tell my past self
10 minutes ago.

Make sure you set an alarm for 5:30am because you got work tomorrow.
Take a shower first then lay down in bed to call her.
Don't start off with a joke about how you were too busy to talk to her, she won't be happy about that and you will regret the whole conversation afterwards.
Do NOT and I repeat, DO NOT say "Calm Down it was a joke".. she will not Calm down.
Remember you needed to check the email she sent you before you call, failure to do this will only cause you more grief.
Remind yourself you love her. You wholeheartedly do... but it won't feel that way in 10 minutes when she begins talking about how you don't pay attention to her issues.
 On that note:
Remember she's had a hard time finding her wedding dress, her grandmother is sick, and she just got her period yesterday.
By the way, FaceTime is a horrible idea. Especially when you know damn well she has the light turned off because it's convenient to say goodnight without having to get up and turn the light off after.
Another thing,
When she says "goodnight" and "I love you", that means you have to say it with the same tone of voice she says it in. Otherwise you will continue talking about why you weren't reciprocating her feelings for you.
Last but not least,
connect your phone to the charging station. You and your phone need to both recharge after that whole ordeal.

A summer in New York

I still remember the warmth of the sun
That day when we first met.
Your voice was familiar to me but your hands were strangers
I've never had the pleasure of knowing until then.
Together we walked those crowded streets
No true destination to arrive at.
We simply desired that sun would not set so we would not have to say goodbye.
It was in the midst of Transit buses, Taxi Cars and Hot dogs stands that we encountered love.
In the most humble, pure and honest form we found joy in each other's presence.
Our Love was brought out by laughter, long gazes, and brief kisses.
At last, all my love was given
 In a summer in New York.

Hurricane Damage

In Florida we get hurricanes.
I grew up knowing when the weatherman says prepare for the storm
That means buying 10 cases of bottled water,
Stocking up on imperishable foods
and board up all your windows.
Don't put tape on the glass, that really doesn't work.
It means get ready for a whole lot of rain and a whole lot of wind.
Something interesting about these storms is that the weatherman give them alphabetical names throughout the year.
A- for Alice
B-For Bernard, so on and so forth.
My worst Hurricane was the one that started with a C…
it's been so long I forgot her name but not the damage she caused me.
That storm swept through my early 20s and took about 5years to finally dissipate in the ocean of my emotional stress.
People told me to prepare but like a lot of folks, I took hurricane warnings lightly.
My heart was a home with no storm shutters,
I was left with no power, my life had no energy to do much after that.
People offered to help with my recovery. It was never the same to say the least
I learned my lesson.
Hurricanes and Heartbreaks should not be taken lightly.

Made in the USA
Columbia, SC
24 April 2021